Manage Stress

2 books in 1

1. Critical Thinking
2. Becomes a Problem Solver

Ray Crystal

Becomes a Problem Solver

A Comprehensive Guide To Learning How To Handle Chaos;

Becomes a Master Problem Solver.

Ray Crystal

Essential Thinking Skills

Tools for Systems Thinkers

Interconnectedness

From linear to circular, systems thinking demands a change in mindset. The shift's principle is that everything is connected. We discuss interconnectedness not in a manner but a biological sciences manner. Everything depends upon something else for survival. Humans and trees need air, food, and sunlight, and carbon dioxide, respectively, to flourish. Everything requires something different, an intricate collection of things, to endure. Inanimate objects will also be reliant on different things: a seat desires a tree to supply its timber to expand, and a mobile phone requires electricity supply. So, once we say 'what's interconnected' out of a system thinking perspective, we're defining a basic existence principle. From this, we could alter how we view the planet from a linear, ordered" mechanical worldview' into a lively, chaotic, interconnected variety of connections and feedback loops. A systems thinker employs this mentality to operate and to entangle inside the complexity of life.

Synthesis

Synthesis refers to make something fresh. The aim is synthesis, instead of analysis into manageable parts, when it comes to systems thinking. Analysis matches into the reductionist and mechanical worldview. However, all programs are dynamic and frequently complex; hence, we need a more holistic understanding. Synthesis is all about knowing the elements and the whole at precisely the same time, in addition to the relationships. Synthesis has the capacity.

Emergence

From a systems standpoint, we all know that bigger things emerge from components: development is the consequence. In the abstract sense, development refers to the universal idea of how life stems from different biological components in varied and unique ways. Emergence is the result of these components' synergies; it's all about nonlinearity and self-organization, and we frequently use the term' development' to characterize the results of things socializing together. A straightforward case of development is a snowflake. It creates components and ecological variables. After the temperature is correct, freezing water particles form in unique fractal patterns around one molecule of thing, including a speck of contamination, a spore, or perhaps dead skin cells. Conceptually, we frequently find development somewhat tricky to get our mind around. Still, once we get it, our mind begins to form emergent results from the different and frequently strange things you experience in the entire world.

Feedback Loops

Since everything is connected, you will find flows and feedback loops between components of a system. When we know dynamics and their kind, we can detect, comprehend, and detract from feedback loops. The two forms of feedback loops are balancing, and both are reinforcing. What may be confusing is that a feedback loop is not a fantastic thing. This occurs when components in a system fortify more like algae growing exponentially in a pond or population growth. A wealth of a single component can refine in strengthening loops. A balancing feedback loop is where things balance out. Nature nearly got this down to a tee with a predator/prey scenario – however, if you take out a lot of a single creature in an ecosystem, the next thing you know, you have a population explosion of a different, that's the other sort of opinions -- strengthening.

Causality

Understanding feedback loops are all about gaining a standpoint of causality: how something contributes to a different thing in a dynamic and continuously evolving platform (all methods are dynamic and always changing somehow; that's the heart of life). Cause and effect are all reasonably common theories in

several professions and life generally --
parents attempt to teach this kind of
crucial life lesson to their young ones,
and I am confident that you can recall a
recent time you're at the forefront of an
effect in an unintentional activity. As a
theory in systems thinking, causality is
about decoding how things affect each
other in a method. Understanding
contributes to a perspective on service,
feedback connections loops, and
relationships, which are parts of systems
mapping.

Systems Mapping

Systems mapping is among the tools of these systems thinkers. There are several approaches to map, from bunch mapping to complex feedback evaluation. On the other hand, principles and the principles of all systems mapping are worldwide. Identify and map the components of things' inside a method to comprehend how they interconnect, link, and behave in an intricate system, and out of here, unique discoveries and insights may be used to create interventions, changes, or coverage decisions that will radically alter the machine in the best way. His introduction into six essential concepts is a crucial building block for creating a more detailed view of how the world functions from a systems standpoint and will improve your ability to think divergently and creatively to get a favorable effect.

Guidelines for Daily Systems Thinking Practice

Individual Practice

Becoming a system thinker begins with a powerful Commitment to creating abilities and awareness.

Ask Unique Question

Systems thinking provide a frame for solving problems in addition to defining issues. To practice thinking out of a systemic standpoint, begin that you ask. Try to ask questions that get at underlying structural connections or patterns of behavior exhibited over time, which concentrate your attention on possible flaws, strengthening or balancing procedures, and unintended consequences, which help you comprehend what periods you are focusing on and how you and others are controlling scenarios.

Learn to Experience Time Differently

When confronted with issues, we're strongly influenced by the messages of society about what constitutes time. We

concentrate on periods that are shorter
than we should.

To fight this, consider that which you're
currently working, making the period
horizon

By way of instance, are you currently
interested in oil prices' behavior since
they go over an interval or a span? What
could be a suitable time horizon for
realizing the effect of disposal?
Additionally, extend your awareness of
exactly what constitutes "the present."

Try thinking concerning a block of time as "currently"--say, one year ago and one year. Ask yourself exactly what happened. What's happening? What does the next year hold? By extending our awareness of "today," we could grasp interconnections we might not have seen previously.

Notice the Systems around You

Consider searching for feedback loops in typical scenarios. By way of instance, has your business started a new product whose sales took off to plateau out? This

may suggest a process that is influenced
by using a procedure. Are you attracted
like a yo-yo involving two extremes? If
this is so, a loop is on the job.

Keep an eye on the effect your actions
have in cycles or your family system
Might there be a loop broken if you
choose your socks up? If the – tap is
turned off while brushing your teeth,
what might happen?

Bring a Loop-a-Day (or just per week).
Each morning sits down with your cup of
coffee, the paper, a pad of paper, and a

pencil, and search for news stories which you could research through causal loop diagrams. Look. (By way of instance, "The unemployment rate climbed over the previous ten decades, as did the number of households looking for welfare support.") Sketch the arrangement which you believe is currently creating these routines. This is a superb way to practice controlling loop diagramming and understanding structures that are systemic. The

Economist magazine is a prosperous

source of systems-oriented stories.

Mental Models

At their most basic level, mental models
explain the thought process one has
regarding the way things in the real-
world work. The relationship between
the various parts of what is being
analyzed and one's actions, feelings,
consequences, etc., are taken into
account to interpret potential
consequences, outcomes, and more.
This is mostly a very detailed breakdown
of a process that occurs quite organically

and seemingly involuntarily. To keep track of mental models, analyze them, and change them is a fundamental part of mastering your mental fortitude and eliminating the barriers that stand between you and what you want in life. When you think about what keeps you from achieving the things you want in life, you will generally find that some combination of your mindset and external circumstances prevented success.

Knowing this, we take another step to unravel that mental process. The more factors we can take control of a situation, the more likely it is to emerge successfully. That makes a fair bit of sense, doesn't it? That's the aim of this writing and the information in it.

What is Mental Model?

A mental model, simply put, is a
representation of the simple mechanics
of something. This is a comprehensive
statement, but mental models are
inherently broad, as you can apply a
model to anything in life. We can't keep
every minute detail of everything we
encounter globally, so these models
simplify the more complex aspects of
life into more digestible and organizable
units.

What are these mental models of which I speak? I'm glad you asked because mental models are the foundation of your entire reality. Understanding them is critical to understanding yourself and your life.

Most people take reality at face value. They assume that life is as they see it. But the reality of reality is that it is subjective, based on each person's unique perception and imagination. A lot of factors go into shaping one's reality.

The result is that no two people see anything the same way.

This leads to a lot of conflict in the world, but it can also lead to poor decisions based on a limited understanding of reality. Mental models are what you use to read reality, and a problematic one can undoubtedly make your life more challenging because it prevents you from seeing reality with clarity.

A mental model is a representation of the human mind's thought process. Mental models are how we understand the world. Not only do they shape what we think and how we understand situations, but they drive our decisions and feelings. They lay the fundamental basis for our lives. What makes mental models tricky is that they are not just influenced by reality – but instead, they draw from a series of experiences, biases, and even a person's current mood. Shaped by culture, personal experiences, and background, they are as unalike as snowflakes from person to person. Two children raised in the same household will have two very different mental models, despite having similar backgrounds and the same culture. Everything that a person sees, hears, and otherwise senses are represented by mental models inside their minds. Mental models are used as scales by which a person automates decisions and internalizes external stimuli. As mentioned by scientists, the Internal scales are ever-changing and unstable as the human mind is susceptible to change due to adaptation. They are also variable since every person has a different outlook and thus a different set of models.

Mental models use perception to drive reasoning and decisions. This reasoning can be flawed at times. Every bit of reasoning you engage in is driven by your perception, no matter how erroneous it may be, as well as dozens or even hundreds of other factors that you may not be aware of.

For example, you may avoid spending time with someone who has a lot of tattoos because you were raised to believe that people with tattoos are lowlifes, but you are not aware of that bias, and you simply dislike someone based on his body modifications. Meanwhile, another person would not have that bias because he was raised differently, so he has no problem hanging out with heavily tattooed people. Your mental model drives you to decide on a person you may not even be consciously aware of.

Furthermore, mental models drive priorities. One woman may consider getting her hair and nails done every few weeks an utmost priority, while another woman does not consider those things necessary at all. Your mental model helps you rate things based on importance so that you can dedicate time, money, and energy to something that you consider worthwhile. Not everyone will agree with your priorities because everyone has a different rating system for importance in life.

Mental models are imperfect because they lack complete information. You can't know everything and focus on everything in the world. You can only focus on a few tiny parts that fit into your accepted reality. Therefore, your lens of reality is relatively narrow, yet it shapes many decisions that can be quite huge.

Think about this example: You support a particular political healthcare proposal because you recognize a few problems, probably problems that affect you personally somehow, with the current system. Your vote this way. However, other people disagree with your accepted healthcare model because they see different problems with the model that you cannot see from your perspective. Thus, you don't understand why people disagree with you, and you feel frustrated.

Your mind will create a small-scale model with the evidence it currently possesses for each situation it encounters. This model will include predicted outcomes of each situation and each decision. Whether or not these outcomes are accurate is hard to say. Sometimes you are right; frequently, you are wrong.

Mental models are paradoxical. Some are quite fluid and change with time and experience. That is why you are a different person now than you were ten years ago, twenty years ago, and so on. You begin to change mental models throughout your life and adapt them to fit what you need. Yet, mental models are also incredibly rigid. Some stay with you for life. Others may be fluid, but your mind relies on them so heavily that it applies them to every area of life, even areas of life that don't benefit from the said mental model.

The takeaway here is that mental models can be changed and adapted to become more helpful. However, you must work hard on your mind to undo years of experience that has created the models.

You must also perform some brutally honest introspection to uncover the real roots of specific thoughts and actions that you routinely engage in. You must be able to let your ego down for a second and say, "Hey, I'm not doing something right. I need to make a change."

Why is this mental work worthwhile? The fact is that your reasoning is not based on logic or rules but rather on mental models. So, if you are operated on a flawed mental model, you are depriving yourself of the ability to use logic to arrive at the ideal decision. Your decisions are influenced in a direction that may not be beneficial in the long run, even though you think they are significant decisions. Learning to recognize mental models and focus on Logic instead can help you make the best decisions for yourself.

Also, since mental models vary from person to person, what works for you may not work for anyone else. This is why your decisions can create a lot of negative conflict within your family, relationship, or team at work. Learning to depend less on mental models can help you arrive at right decisions for everyone involved. This can help you become a better spouse, parent, and leader. It can also help you remove the emotion from decisions, which can lessen the pain of compromising a decision. Since all relationships contain many compromises, you will do better in life if you can accept compromise.

Unforced Errors

An unforced error is a mistake or wrong decision that somehow harms you. In sports, the mistake is often attributed to your failure rather than the talent of the opponent. For example, if you goof at a tennis match, you may blame yourself for not playing the right way when you were up against a better tennis player. The fewer unforced errors you make in life, the better off you are. You can avoid making grave errors at work or in your family. You can avoid entering unhealthy relationships or losing lots of money. Things are great in life when you make wise, informed decisions.

Mental models are designed to help you avoid unforced errors. Using a first bias model, people tend to operate on loss aversion, or to prevent losses, rather than using their skills for the maximum potential benefit. Thus, most people have a built-in loss aversion model that drives them to make decisions in life, as represented by athletes' sports decisions. This model is not ideal; however, using your maximum utility skills and focusing

on making right decisions instead of

minimizing losses is a better use of your

energy.

Your brain has intuition, and nine times

out of ten, that intuition is wrong. Many

of our instincts no longer serve us, yet

they run in the background, driving us to

make decisions that don't make a lot of

logical sense. It is wise to use your

brain's intuition and mental models to

guide life, not an instructional manual. If

you have an intuitive response to a

situation, be sure to check out your intuition with Logic before committing to the decision.

Since the brain loves to formulate predictions, you often think you know how something will go. You then base your decision off of that assumption to avoid an unforced error. However, life is seldom predictable. Take your assumptions as hypotheses, not reality.

Solving Problems and Decision-Making

Traditionally speaking, we have been taught to solve a problem linearly, moving neatly from Roman numeral I to Point A. But with systems thinking, there is an acknowledgment that this isn't really how the world works: the world is messy and intertwined and unpredictable in many ways. Systems thinking urges us to look at the bigger picture, rather than the multiple components of the smaller problems and events that plague us each day. This big-picture thinking helps us to envision better solutions for complex issues.

When we talk about systems in general, we can be referring to any number of concepts, such as environmental, economic, political, social, and familial. Each of these concepts, in turn, interacts and merges to create larger systems that shape our lives: markets are created out of economic forces, both actual (companies, infrastructure) and intangible (stocks, trade regulations) coupled with political governance and social needs and desires, for example. If we simply look at a market via one conceptual lens, then we are not well equipped to understand it or to function successfully within it.

Think of the adage about teaching a man to fish. The traditional saying goes like, "I give a man a fish, and he eats for a day; if you teach a man to fish, and he eats for a lifetime." While there is something that strikes us as

fundamentally correct in that saying—
teaching skill is undoubtedly a longer-
term solution to the problem—systems
thinking requires that we look at a bigger
picture. Why might the above response
be inadequate?

Various other factors are present within
the bigger picture. For instance, what if
there aren't enough fish left in the water
source because of climate change? What
if the water is polluted from the activities
of corporations or individuals? Who
controls access to the lake, influential

individuals, corporate entities, or public sources? How does the hungry man afford to buy the materials necessary to catch the fish? On the other side, what about the opportunities for expansion? Is there a local market for extra fish the man may pick? Could this be a chance at a more significant and longer-term investment?

The fact of the matter is that any of these above scenarios could occur in the bigger picture, and teaching a man to fish is only the tip of the iceberg There are all sorts of external factors that determine how adequate that response might be, not to mention personal limitations and opportunities. Systems thinking recognize that the man in this scenario, not to mention the fish, is only one small part of a much larger ecological, economic, and political universe. Acknowledging that helps us to make smarter decisions for how to create opportunities while also protecting resources.

The current challenges we face in a global world demand new and more complex answers, which requires new ways of looking at old ideas. Investing in a fossil fuel company may not be the long-term success story it once was. Relying on government intervention alone to protect resources and maintain social justice may no longer be feasible. Not to mention the straightforward fact that the above scenario changes significantly if we set the scene in, say, sub-Saharan Africa or if we consider that the fisherman might be a fisherwoman.

The environmental and social challenges,

not to slight the political, will differ

depending on the scenario. It behooves

us to examine the system and understand

all the intricacies of its many dynamic

parts.

Some of the benefits of systems—or

bigger picture—thinking is that it

encourages us to think outside of our

unique skill set. We need to face

challenges with multi-disciplinary zeal

(which begs the question about how we

educate our young adults to enter the workforce—a book in and of itself). It also, paradoxically, encourages us to make incremental rather than sweeping changes; we learn from small changes (and mistakes) and adapt accordingly. It is a more flexible way in which to approach complex problems. As we can see from the teach a man to fish analogy above, even what seems like the most straightforward problem is fraught with complex issues.

In systems thinking, there is also the implicit understanding that solving problems is not like old-style imperial conquest: you don't head off into the "wilderness" and suggest to those living and working there that your way of thinking and doing is "right" or better. Looking at the bigger picture requires considering local actors, whether they be workers or colleagues, consumers, or villagers. This kind of thinking involves facilitation, empowering localized ownership, and responsibility. This is reminiscent of some old stories—

perhaps apocryphal—told about the early

British colonials. In one story,

missionaries descended upon an African

village and, upon meeting the locals,

were embarrassed and a bit horrified by

their lack of what a nineteenth-century

preacher would consider adequate

clothing. So, they imported enough

woolen suits for the men and long

dresses for the women. The Africans,

wishing to get along with the

missionaries (who, one must not forget,

were armed to the teeth), adopted the new clothes—and wore them throughout the monsoon season, with its soaking rains and soaring heat. Many villagers feel ill, and some perished. Another story, related by Jared Diamond in Guns, Germs, and Steel, talks about how colonial farmers ended up settling near waterways in Africa: this makes sense in England, where waterways provide both food and water; but in Africa, waterways are dangerous, fierce housing animals and—ultimately more deadly—large populations of mosquitoes that transmitted malaria. Before the discovery of quinine, untold numbers of settlers died of the disease. Imposing will on or ignoring wisdom from local entities is almost always disastrous.

Essentially, the more contemporary saying "act locally, think globally" could easily apply to the goals of systems thinking. Making localized changes while also revamping the system itself to be more productive and inclusive is the ideal use for more significant picture thinking. We look beyond immediate problems to long-term solutions and mobilize people from many different sectors, adapting and responding to feedback loops along the way. In the end, whether professionally or personally, this kind of thinking makes a winner out of everyone involved.

Managing Chaos

Chaos Theory is concerned with explaining non-linearity in the development of systems. Analyses that are based upon a single cause seeking a single effect are linear. Non-linearity represents unpredictable change. Change, in turn, means that a system is dynamic. Lack of change denotes a static system. Systems rarely operate in a steady-state and progress in a linear fashion. A linear system is deterministic;

its outcomes can be predicted from the initial conditions, cause, and effect. However, it is much more common for the form of a system to change unpredictably. As a system, a tree will develop from seed to seedling, from sapling to maturity, old age, limb loss, and die back. Its general form or genotype will be mostly predictable, but its specific shape or phenotype will not. Indeed, every tree, although similar within species, will be different. No two trees, dogs, cats, cows, landscapes, cloud

formations, snowflakes in a snowstorm,
or people on earth will be the same. A
car will run well when new, but over
time, paint fades, rust will invade,
bearings will wear out, and parts will
fail. No two old cars, even of the same
make and model, will be the same. A
perusal of quality and prices of stock of
secondhand car dealers will suffice to
prove this point.

Similarly, a human will change over
his/her lifetime as youthful strength and
agility may decline. Still, thinking and

rational capacity may increase until all sub-systems break down in old age. Therefore, systems do not move through time with precisely the same shape as when they commenced. If they made it, their progress would be linear. But systems development is non-linear. The development of Chaos theory helps to explain non-linearity.

Chaos does not represent disorder. Instead it explains that there is the order in what at first sight appears to be disorder. Each tree in the forest is different, representing disorder, but the differences lie within predictable bounds as each one is recognizably a tree. This represents the order in the seeming disorder. The characteristics of Chaos are:

- Sensitivity to initial conditions (as mentioned above about system creation) leads to unpredictability.

- Mixing in which adjacent points may end up in entirely different positions as the system progresses.

- Non-linearity as the output of one system becomes the input to the preceding one.

- Feedback is a significant driver of Chaos.

The concept of increasing order within a system may be traced to Descartes. Descartes held that the ordinary laws of nature would bring about order and that an external guiding hand was unnecessary.

A feature of systems is wholeness. But paradoxically, within the wholeness lies

further complexity as systems are formed
of sub-systems. While these sub-systems
are 'whole,' they, in turn, are
components of the larger system. And
not only are the more extensive system
components, but they often do not have a
viable independent existence and are in
themselves composed of further
subordinate sub-systems. For example,
the trunk of a tree is an essential
component of the system that is a tree
but, once removed, ceases to function
independently. The sub-system of the

tree trunk consists of subordinate sub-systems of Bark to provide protection, Phloem to supply sap from leaves to branches and roots, Cambium to provide new cells for the phloem, Xylem to move water and minerals up the tree to the leaves, and Heartwood that consists of old Xylem and provides support and strength. Each of these can be analyzed down the level of the individual cells that comprise them. The same analysis may be conducted with a cow's liver or the gearbox of a motor car. They exist in themselves but are, in turn, comprised of further sub-systems. The origins of the word system can be seen: 'system' is Latin for a whole consisting of several parts. Therefore, a system is a group of components that interact to form an integrated entity or whole.

An economy is a system as it takes in raw materials, transforms them by production processes into goods and services, and distributes them for consumption. Therefore, the Economic System analysis involves studying the

production, exchange, and consumption
of goods and services. The economic
system's foundation structure may be
depicted in its broad sub-system
components of production, exchange,
and consumption.

Creating Lasting Solutions

Traditionally speaking, we have been taught to solve a problem linearly, moving neatly from Roman numeral I to Point A. But with systems thinking, there is an acknowledgment that this isn't really how the world works: the world is messy and intertwined and unpredictable in many ways. Systems thinking urges us to look at the bigger picture, rather than the multiple components of the smaller problems and events that plague us each day. This big-picture thinking helps us to envision better solutions for complex issues.

When we talk about systems in general, we can be referring to any number of concepts, such as environmental, economic, political, social, and familial. Each of these concepts, in turn, interacts and merges to create larger systems that shape our lives: markets are created out of economic forces, both actual (companies, infrastructure) and intangible (stocks, trade regulations) coupled with political governance and social needs and desires, for example. If we simply look at a market via one conceptual lens, we cannot understand it or function successfully.

Think of the adage about teaching a man to fish. The traditional saying goes like, "I give a man a fish, and he eats for a day; if you teach a man to fish, and he eats for a lifetime." While there is something that strikes us as fundamentally correct in that saying— teaching skill is undoubtedly a longer-term solution to the problem—systems thinking requires that we look at a bigger picture. Why might the above response be inadequate?

Various other factors are present within the bigger picture. For instance, what if there aren't enough fish left in the water source because of climate change? What if the water is polluted from the activities of corporations or individuals? Who controls access to the lake, influential individuals, corporate entities, or public sources? How does the hungry man afford to buy the materials necessary to catch the fish? On the other side, what about the expansion opportunities? Is there a local market for extra fish the man may pick? Could this be a chance at a more significant and longer-term investment?

The fact of the matter is that any of these above scenarios could occur in the bigger picture, and teaching a man to fish is only the tip of the iceberg. There are all sorts of external factors that determine how adequate that response might be, not to mention personal limitations and opportunities. Systems thinking recognizes that the man in this scenario, not to mention the fish, is only one small part of a much larger ecological, economic, and political universe. Acknowledging that helps us to make smarter decisions for how to create opportunities while also protecting resources.

The current challenges we face in a global world demand new and more complex answers, which requires new ways of looking at old ideas. Investing in a fossil fuel company may not be the long-term success story it once was. Relying on government intervention alone to protect resources and maintain social justice may no longer be feasible. Not to mention the straightforward fact that the above scenario changes significantly if we set the scene in, say, sub-Saharan Africa or if we consider that the fisherman might be a fisherwoman. The environmental and social challenges, not to slight the political, will differ depending on the scenario. It behooves us to examine the system and understand all the intricacies of its many dynamic parts.

One of the benefits of systems—or more significant picture—thinking is that it encourages us to think outside of our unique skill set. We need to face challenges with multi-disciplinary zeal (which begs how we educate our young adults to enter the workforce—a book in and of itself). Paradoxically, it encourages us to make incremental rather than sweeping changes; we learn from small changes (and mistakes) and adapt accordingly. It is a more flexible way in which to approach complex problems. As we can see from the teach a man to fish analogy above, even what seems like the most straightforward problem is fraught with complex issues. In systems thinking, there is also the implicit understanding that solving problems is not like old-style imperial conquest: you don't head off into the "wilderness" and suggest to those living and working there that your way of thinking and doing is "right" or better. Looking at the bigger picture requires considering local actors, whether they be workers or colleagues, consumers, or villagers. This kind of thinking involves facilitation, empowering localized ownership, and responsibility. This is reminiscent of some old stories—perhaps apocryphal—told about the early British colonials. In one story, missionaries descended upon an African village and, upon meeting the locals, were embarrassed and a bit horrified by their lack of what a nineteenth-century preacher would consider adequate clothing. So, they imported enough woolen suits for the men and long dresses for the women. The Africans, wishing to get along with the missionaries (who, one must not forget, were armed to the teeth), adopted the new clothes—and wore them throughout the monsoon season, with its soaking rains and soaring heat. Many villagers feel ill, and some perished. Another story, related by Jared Diamond in Guns, Germs, and Steel, talks about how colonial farmers ended up settling near waterways in Africa: this makes sense in England, where waterways provide both food and water; but in Africa, waterways are dangerous, fierce housing animals and—ultimately more deadly—large populations of mosquitoes that transmitted malaria. Before the discovery of quinine, untold numbers of settlers died of the disease. Imposing will on or ignoring wisdom from local entities is almost always disastrous.

The newer saying "act locally, think globally" could easily apply to systems thinking goals. Making localized changes while also revamping the system itself to be more productive and inclusive is ideal for more significant picture thinking. We look beyond immediate problems to long-term solutions and mobilize people from many different sectors, adapting and responding to feedback loops along the way. In the end, whether professionally

or personally, this kind of thinking

makes a winner out of everyone

involved.

Critical Thinking

Forms You Thought; This Guide Will Teach You How To Create Your Own Personal Thinking

Ray Crystal

Critical Thinking

Critical thinking helps us with different data.

It may help us think. One way to approach thinking is through the Analysis of Logic--such as formal Logic (which assembles decisions almost mathematically (with syllogisms), simple Logic (which also considers material, context, and delivery), and fuzzy Logic (which admits that lots of attributes are subjective or topics of level).

Critical thinking provides us with strategies to think through data and a way to decide which opinions are important. One might manipulate data to change information in various ways. In fact, computer programs change data. Yet some would argue that manipulation brings an uncertain kind of knowledge.

There's always further information related to data, and these issues have various meanings. Information could have various purposes.

One of the most important aspects perhaps is that data doesn't decide anything, but instead models our understanding.

Another important aspect is that data is merely information, not knowledge. Another aspect of data is that it's useless if we can't deal with the information. Yet another important aspect is that data's seriousness stays steady, remaining above fluff and gossip.

This story is a rational story. Scientists are logical. Critical thinkers will also find it logical. Yet, not everybody thinks rationally.

Rational thoughts may not be free. Rational thought may be the consequence of skills acquired, like any other skills. We use skills because we need them, for example in a functional life. Critical thinking counts more than critical analysis.

In this story, there are many questions, not all of which have concrete answers, although we may try to understand what all those data mean.

In fact, the story raises many questions, because questions create wonder and self-reflection.

A critical thinker asks questions, but also uses barriers to excess curiosity. That is, a critical thinker lets the data speak, and doesn't try to put the information into an uneasy package where it doesn't fit. A few data are like a weak light in a dark room.

This is a story about other options people often don't consider.

One character takes one particular option. He is alone in seeking it, and it isn't always so clear what he is seeking. He is a clear, creative thinker who questions the anomalous. He is a philosopher-scientist.

This story is concerned with some of the stuff philosophy and science have considered. Still, we may need to discover what's essential for a creative life on earth.

The character in this story is often lonely, but he doesn't mind. In fact, it's his solitude that allows his mind to work.

This character has the courage to think the unusual and the skill to dwell on the questions and ideas his critical thinking produces. One character talks of him in these words: "Well done, John. Well done. I'm surprised at your insight. I'm doubly surprised, your insight is original.

Very few people come up with ideas like this one. You have a unique mind. I'm impressed—John.

" In general, the character in this story is an original genius. But, he understands that his ideas haven't prevailed, and he's aware of history.

The character in this story seems unusual. In fact, the character may seem at first to avoid traditional goals in life. In the end, the character does achieve what he's after.

The character receives acclaim for his work. The character works hard throughout the story, as the story itself demonstrates. For this reason, his goal of reasoning may seem worthwhile because pieces of it show up in different places. Also, he's been successful in his speech, because he's well-spoken. He's articulate.

This is a story of a rational man, a man who thinks at length and with clarity. He answers his questions, and also makes questions. He gives answers, and presents new questions. This man with a unique mind struggles to achieve the clarity of mind which is his dream.

This story provides data, not just its usual telling of a story. Challenging, original data makes up the story, like most of the things we care to know about.

When we think, we're not only logical in how we do it, but also creative, and critical, and even emotional. We think with our imagination. And such thoughts may go in unexpected directions. Science is a good example of how to be logical and inventive.

Critical thinking is a way to development insight. Philosophy allows us to think. Our minds need more than we often give them. This is a story of one man who thinks. This man thinks a lot. He doesn't mind being alone. This man thinks.

He thinks the impossible, too. He considers things like teleportation and how to know what will happen in certain situations. This man who thinks and thinks and thinks has a passion for thinking.

In the end, we see this man is a free thinker who often sees things in new ways, and he enjoys his work in cryptography and also general research.

More than anything else, this man thinks. He thinks about the science that surrounds him. And he thinks about life. He thinks about the future. He thinks about time and about how the future and the past exist in different kinds of ways.

He thinks about time travel, too, including what it's like and how it might be possible. He also thinks about philosophy, and about critical thinking itself. He thinks about anomalous data, and he thinks about data itself. He thinks about the nature of data.

Are data changing as they age, over time?

What is Critical Thinking?

Critical thinking can be defined as thinking and being rational about your beliefs or what to do. It involves the ability of one to engage in independent and reflective thinking. A person with critical thinking skills should be able to do the following:

- Objectively reflect on why their beliefs and values are justified;

- Systematically solve problems;

- Understand the connection between ideas logically;

- Identify, construct, understand, and analyze arguments;

- Identify inconsistent mistakes in reasoning;

and Understand the importance and relevance of ideas.

Critical thinking can also be described as the skill to analyze facts to conclude logically.

It involves careful consideration of information established as accurate, clearly outlining a rational process of thought about that information, and objectively arriving at a judgment.

If that last paragraph sounds complicated, the good news is that you have probably already engaged in some form of critical thinking.

If you want to purchase a new car and know what you want regarding the car's price, condition, quality, and features, you have to compare several different car models. You might read several reviews about a particular car that seems like the right one.

You'll collect more information about that specific car. If it fits your criteria, you'll then compare sellers in terms of their pricing and customer feedback to find a seller that you can trust to give you the right car at a reasonable price.

Along the way, you'll make sure that the reviews you are reading come from reliable sources that honestly describe the car and the seller (rather than old reviews that may no longer reflect current conditions, reviews that don't explain anything, or biased reviews that might not reflect an accurate assessment). Once you have analyzed the facts, you find the right car model and seller and ultimately make your purchase.

You just used a form of critical thinking to purchase a car. You had a clear purpose (finding a car), you came up with a solution (you decided which model of the car you wanted to buy), you used information (reviews) while carefully determining which information was truthful and useful (only using reviews you trusted), analyzed that information, and solved your problem (you now have a new car).

You did NOT merely pick a car that looked nice in the photographs and went to the first car dealership you found one random day. You also didn't just take every review at face value or buy a specific car because someone told you to buy that one.

You not only thought about your decision and used the information to come to it, but you also thought about why you were making that particular choice and put some thought into the information in front of you.

Of course, sifting through all of those reviews, prices, and feedback is time-consuming and not always straightforward. Suppose you are trying to decide upon which political candidate to vote for, which college you should attend, or some other decision that may involve your own personal values, the process of critical thinking can be even more complicated. In that case, thus, this book will help you understand critical thinking as a tool for everyday life as well as the "big questions" you may come across.

It is important to note that critical thinking is not about the accumulation of information. If a person has an excellent memory or is aware of many facts, it does not mean that they are critical thinkers.

A critical thinker is an individual that can realize the consequences from the information they have and understands how to effectively use the information they have to solve problems and seek

more relevant information to stay
informed.

Being argumentative or critical of others
is now what critical thinking is all about.
Critical thinking skills can be used to
point out fallacies and wrong reasoning
and play a role in joint reasoning and
constructive improvements and tasks.
Critical thinking can also be used to
improve work processes and enhance
social institutions.

It has been argued that critical thinking
obstructs creativity because it involves
following the rules of rationality and
logic, while creativity may involve
breaking the same rules.

However, this is not true. Critical
thinking is very compatible with many
aspects of creative thinking.

In essence, critical thinking is an
essential part of creativity, as we require

critical thinking to evaluate and enhance creative ideas.

Skills in Critical Thinking

Critical thinking is a lifelong process that even the most profound thinkers continuously practice and refine further.

Think about the following skills less like something you can just suddenly perfect and more like habits of mind that you'll always take with you—habits that will improve over time. Regardless of your origin or background, it is essential to have critical thinking skills.

The lack of such skills can break one's career due to the inability to understand and analyze information effectively.

In this era of immense competition, critical thinking skills are more critical than ever before. According to Kris Potrafka, everything is at risk—thus the need to think more critically. Lack of critical thinking will lessen your chances of climbing the ladder in your career or industry of choice.

In order not to succumb to such, it is essential to develop your skills in critical thinking. However, it is essential first to understand what those skills are to know how to improve or enhance them.
There are no universal standards for the skills required in critical thinking, but in this section, we shall discuss six of them:

Identification

Firstly, you need to determine what's wrong and what influenced this to happen.
Only through understanding your circumstance can you solve your problem.
Once you have identified the problem or situation, you need to stop and take a mental inventory of

what is going on as you inquire:

What is being done?
What caused your situation?
What will likely happen?

Research

When comparing the different aspects of a situation or an issue, uninfluenced research ability is essential. Arguments must be convincing. This means that the figures and facts presented may be lacking in context or are not credible.

To help with this, verify the unsourced claims. Is the person bringing the argument offering their source of information? If you ask and there is no clear answer, that should serve as a warning. Learn to verify the sources of any information and its authenticity.

Identify biases

This is a difficult skill. It is not easy to recognize a bias, yet it is very crucial in critical thinking. Strong critical thinkers must be objective in evaluating the information they receive. Take the assumption that you are a judge required to listen to both sides and keep in mind the biases on both sides.

Of equal importance, however, if not more, is learning how you must set aside your own biases so that your judgment is impartial. Learn to debate and argue with your thoughts and perceptions.

This is important as a skill because it enables you to see things from different viewpoints.

Always assess your source of information and challenge the evidence that forms your beliefs. You must always be aware of the existence of biases.

As you analyze any information or argument, it is essential to ask yourself the following questions:

Who benefits?

The source of information—is it credible, or does it have a hidden agenda?
Is the source biased and overlooks details proving them wrong?
Is it persuasive enough to let make people believe?

Inference

The ability to internalize and make conclusions based on available information is also essential in mastering critical thinking. Most of the information won't mean it as is.

As a critical thinker, you will often need to analyze the information presented and come up with conclusions based on raw data.

It is not easy to infer. An inference is an informed guess, and the ability to correctly infer can be enhanced by consciously making an effort to collect as much information as you possibly can before you jump to conclusions.

Determine Relevance

Critical thinking can be very challenging when figuring out what information is most relevant to analyze. In many cases, you may be presented with information that may seem very important only to realize that it is a minor point to consider.

The best solution to determine relevance is to first understand what is expected.

Have you been asked to find a solution? Should you understand the trend?

When you understand what is expected from the situation, it becomes much easier to know what is relevant and what is not.

Another tip to determining the relevance of information is by making a list of data points that you rank to be relevant.

In doing this, you will likely have a list containing relevant information at the top of the list and not so important information down. Then, trim down these details and put your attention to what's relevant.

Curiosity

It is a more comfortable choice to accept every piece of information presented at face value. However, this can be disastrous when faced with a situation that requires thinking critically. Every human being is naturally curious. Don't allow the impulse to ask questions to die because that is not the way of critical thinkers.

Train yourself to be productively curious. Asking insightful questions about your daily reality necessitates mindfulness, and it's a vital ability you must acquire as a critical thinker.

Critical Thinking for

Change your Life

Critical thinking is an ability that can be applied to every area of one's everyday life. You might be shocked at the decisions you can, will, and have made, requiring you to think critically before following through.

Critical thinking is more than logic and reason.

It is also a process of information gathering, which involves gathering and assessing information and thinking about your thinking.

"Critical thinking" is actually a very simple process, but it's also a very powerful one. You are the user of critical thinking; you are its instrument. There is a critical thinking method; every critical thinker uses and employs it in his or her own way.

People actually think critically and use critical thinking without realizing it. Sometimes we call it "enlightened common sense."

We all regularly asked to think critically in our lives. Important decisions await our judgment and our action; time for reflection is short. Critical thinking is a skill that can help us to deal with such cases and situations.

The skill of critical thinking will allow us to better solve problems, deal with irrational and ill-advised decisions, and make better, more informed, decisions in all areas of our lives. Let's try to understand what critical thinking is.

To understand what critical thinking is, let's first talk about what it is not. Critical thinking is not brain surgery, and it is not a discipline taught in school.

Consider, for example, what is required to be a neurosurgeon:

You must spend years of study and training.

With this formalized training you will develop a complex expertise.

In comparison, a skill in critical thinking has a different history.

There is no formal training regimen or certification process.

This skill is basically a skill of the mind, but it must rely on at least two disciplines for its creation, training, and development.

Those two disciplines are logic and philosophy.

It takes both logic and philosophy to train the mind to think critically. It doesn't have to be through formal education, but that's the best way to learn.

Consider the following as a definition of critical thinking:
 "Critical thinking is a skill for identifying biases in the way you think that can cause you to reach invalid conclusions."
Armed with a skill in critical thinking You can perform critical thinking at any time.

A lot of people have questioned the efficiency of critical thinking, ranging from people who haven't read about it or experienced it and think it is just a bunch of book-learning, to people who have read about it and seen how effective it can be, but cannot apply it in their lives.

This is due to lack of practice and skills in this area. Critical thinking is not as easy to learn as some other skills are. It does take practice, but the more you practice, the easier it becomes.

Improvement in one's critical thinking skills does not have to be slow or difficult.

We not only need to know what critical thinking is, we need to know what it is not. The skill has been greatly misunderstood, and it has been severely underestimated.

Some say that it is a concept taught in classrooms. That is not true.

Critical thinking is a skill that is needed throughout everyday life. Our daily lives often present us with opportunities to judge and make decisions.

It is quite easy to make a poor decision, requiring us to waste time and money, because of bias or haste.

Critical thinking can be used just to make life easier and easier. It does not take much time or effort, but the results are often impressive.

Critical thinking allows us to approach a problem without bias.

In other words, we want to become an impartial decision maker who is considering all the evidence before making a decision, even if we might not have all the necessary facts. Critical thinking allows us to make wiser and more informed decisions.

I expect that you will be involved in some of these decisions. You might find yourself making a very important decision, perhaps one that will have a direct impact on the rest of your life, such as choosing a college, choosing a life partner, business partner, or even a friend.

Maybe you're just making a snap judgment. With critical thinking, you can make the best decision without resorting to snap judgments. Critical thinking leads us to a judgment that will be based on careful reasoning.

It will be the best decision until new information is collected that causes you to change your decision.

Critical thinking gives us the chance to make the best informed decision. Our decisions must be based on the judgments that result from careful reasoning. Further, your judgment must consider all the relevant arguments.

Critical Reading

Learning to read critically involves actively participating in what we read, first developing a clear understanding of the author's ideas, then challenging and evaluating the arguments and evidence provided to support those arguments, and finally forming our points of view. In this way, reading requires us to develop skills that are not necessary for more passive forms of information retrieval.
Steps for Critical Reading:

- Before reading, scan the piece to get an idea of what it is and the main argument. It can include reading an introduction, if available, or captions.

- As you read, continue an ongoing dialogue with the author through comments, recording your thoughts, ideas, and questions. Underline, feature, or circle significant parts and points and compose remarks in the margins.

- After reading, check their remarks to get an overall thought of the content. You can likewise decide to write a summary to improve your comprehension.

- If you react to the text after you have built up a clear sense of the author's argument and thinking, you can dissect the author's argument and techniques. At that point, you can build up your thoughts, perhaps in your display.

Reading critically means that the reader is always thinking. The reader makes judgment calls about what is going on in the text by asking questions.

They notice clues and make inferences. A reader who is critical can figure out what the author's purpose is and how the writer is using language to persuade the reader to do something.

When a person reads a text, they're looking for the main purpose of the text. A critical reader asks questions that help them figure out where the author is going with the text. Just like a detective, a critical reader asks questions and looks for clues.

Clues are pieces of information an author has put into the text. Critical readers look for clues in the beginning of the text because usually the beginning will give clues about what's coming up.

The ending of the story provides clues about what is to come. Reading critically means that the reader is always thinking. This gives the reader the opportunity to make predictions about what is going to happen.

For example, they are thinking:

"Based on this information, I'm guessing what the next event is going to be."

A critical reader asks questions that let them see their hunches were right or wrong.

Questions that a critical reader asks can be about details, logical thoughts, or about the author's purpose. Critical readers
Critical reading is the process of doing close reading of a text, known as a text analysis. When doing a text analysis, the reader is looking for certain details in the text. Critical reading is hard work. A person who does a text analysis looks for details that help show the author's purpose.

The person who is doing an analysis tries to figure out the writer's purpose for writing the text.
In this story the main purpose of the writing is to entertain the reader. The story has several points and each point adds to this main purpose.

This story is an adventure story with a great plot and strong characters. This story will keep the reader actively involved, and encourage the reader to keep reading until the end.

Once the student has read the story and asked the questions, they will be ready to answer the questions by an analysis of the story. The kind of questions that a critical reader asks will help to create the analysis. Once the reader has read the story, they will create an initial draft of their analysis.

The initial draft is a first draft. It is a rough draft to get the main ideas out.

Once the main ideas are out, they should try to refine it. This is the process of getting the ideas and making them fit together in a logical way.

They may make changes to the draft along the way. If they have questions about parts of the draft, they will ask someone who is familiar with the story, perhaps the teacher or an older sibling. They will ask these people if the draft makes sense.

Personal experiences are an important key to making the draft better. Personal experiences are things that relate to how the person feels towards the story.

The reader can use them
if the person reads, enjoys reading, if the plot of the story is relatable, and if the character in the story

Critical Writing

Writing critically is very important in academic writing. In your English classes, you will be asked to write at least one argumentative paper that will ask you to defend one side or another. Critical writing can be broken down.

To put it merely, critical writing evaluates and analyzes more than one source to develop an argument. This is different than descriptive writing, which describes what something is like. However, a description will be involved in your critical writing, along with an explanation.

There should be a right balance between analysis and description. Critical thinking will make your writing clearer and more concise.

This allows you to make well-thought-out arguments in a shorter amount of time with more success. Being transparent will increase readability. This will allow for a wider audience and a more enjoyable read.

When writing, sometimes it is difficult to put your thoughts on paper without sounding crazy. Being told to write more clearly is a lot easier than actually writing clearly. Therefore, this is going to give you a few tips and pointers on becoming a better writer.

At this point, you have heard a lot about how to think critically, cognitive biases, and how to escape the trap Groupthink creates. Now, you will be able to write critically. When you are writing critically, you'll be able to word your thoughts better, and your paragraphs will be more useful – it won't just be about word counts anymore, but the word counts will be met regardless.

The following is a series of questions you can ask. These can be applied to writing and editing your writing:

- Is your idea/argument a good or bad one?

- Is my argument valid and defensible? Is it the opposite?

- We have talked about how to determine whether an argument is valid, but you also need to defend your argument with premises and supporting details. If you cannot do this, your perspective will be easy to poke holes in and collapse like a house of cards.

- The reason is something we have already talked about quite a bit. It is crucial because it will justify your position.

Stereotypes are not foolproof; therefore, they should not be used in an argument because there are many instances where they will not be valid. The same goes for clichés. Clichés are overused and only occur in a perfect situation.

Do I touch more profound points, or do I only scrape the surface when talking about my topic?
Go into detail! Details are so important, and the better support you have for your argument, the better.

Don't be repetitive, but present as many different details as possible, especially in the first draft of your writing. You should strive to understand what you are writing about and encourage your readers to understand what they are reading.

Do I address the other points of view adequately?

Always consider the counterarguments. These will test your own viewpoint, and those who support the counterarguments will be looking for things that will take your argument down.
Do I question my ideas and test them for validity?

Question all of the evidence you find and make sure things like experiments and observation support it. If there are surveys involved in your argument, make sure the pool of people surveyed is an accurate proportion.

Create a goal and write it down. This will help you stick with the purpose of your argument.
When forming an argument and writing about it, you will need to give yourself time and be very organized.

Your first step should be to research. Utilize all outlets that you have access to. Go to the library and read as much as you can about your topic first and write down important points and supporting details.

Then, if you have access to any online databases, use those. Generally, depending on your topic, you will find statistics and experiments. Do not disregard anything because it does not directly address your viewpoint.

Anything you can learn is good. The more you broaden your knowledge on the topic, the easier it will be for you to argue one way or another. You never know – halfway through, you may discover that you think the opposing viewpoint is better.

Once you have searched databases, go to the search engines, and you will find the opinions of others and some more supporting details. The more information that you have and know about a topic, the easier your thoughts will flow.

At this point, you should have several more sources than what is required. In the end, you will have to cut down the number of sources because you should not need them all.

Next, you should make outlines. That's right, multiple. Each should get more detailed, and by the end, you will have a sentence outline. This is essentially your first draft with different numbers and sections.

You may think that making multiple outlines is excessive, but it will allow you to see your information in several different ways.

When you look at the information in the same font in block paragraphs, it is difficult to determine whether it will be apparent to readers. This is why having someone else edit it is essential.

Furthermore, if you don't have someone else, as long as you have given yourself enough time, you can put the project away and look at it the next day.

Your writing should not be confusing or full of hidden meaning. Make it as straightforward as possible. When you go through and edit, you should determine whether the following questions are easily found:

Is the purpose of the piece clear and easily found?

Stating the purpose in the first paragraph is the easiest way to do this. You are not trying to conceal your topic.

There is no harm in including it in some of your first thoughts.

What questions does this piece answer?

What questions are explored?

From what perspective is my argument?

You should know this for a couple of different reasons.

Understanding your perspective will allow you to write about it clearer.

It will also allow you to determine the opposing viewpoints and determine counterarguments.

Where did I get my information? Are the sources valid? Was the information consistent in all of my sources?

What concepts are central in my line of thinking?

These would be your main points, a standard number of main points is three, but you can have any number of main points to support your argument.

These main points will have supporting details. They can be considered the premises of your arguments.

What conclusions am I making? What premises do I include?

These, of course, would be your entire argument.

If you use a thesis statement, which you should, your premises and conclusions will be found here.

Your thesis statement will only feature your premises and your conclusion.

Write the premises in the order that they will appear to make the thesis statement more usable.

Am I making any assumption/s? Are these assumptions that I should be making?

There is a difference between making an educated inference and just making assumptions.

For example, if there are no clouds in the sky, we can assume it will not rain.

However, just because George Clooney is not your father does not mean you can assume he is your best friend's father.

You must have evidence to support this.

As a writer who writes critically, you should be able to evaluate your work thoroughly. The questions above will help you with this.

While you write, you will use several different thinking levels: validity, context, accuracy, and precision. The conclusions you make should be predictable when paired with all of the evidence you gathered.
Always keep your argument reasonable, stable, and valid. Besides, you should always consider any weaknesses your argument has, along with potential counterarguments.

How does considering counterarguments help you?

Well, you will be able to strengthen your argument by pointing out the weaknesses in the counterarguments.

You can also block the holes in your argument by strategizing and using critical thinking. Make your weaknesses seem like strengths in an argument.

Writing is essential and can help you think critically successfully.

Writing requires you to do two things:

write out your thoughts entirely and make them readable to a varied audience.

Thinking critically is like speaking proper English to someone who learned it as a second language.

You may be introducing a concept entirely new for your audience.

This requires you to be extremely thorough, and you must know your topic thoroughly.

Your awareness of a topic will increase when you write it out, and complex problems can be worked through and solved.

Ray Crystal